1997

GIFTS OF THE SPIRIT:
MULTIPLE INTELLIGENCES IN RELIGIOUS EDUCATION

BY REV. RONALD NUZZI, PhD

NATIONAL CATHOLIC EDUCATIONAL ASSOCIATION

ISBN 1-55833-181-6

TABLE OF CONTENTS

ABOUT THE AUTHOR

ev. Ronald J. Nuzzi is a priest of the Diocese of Youngstown Ohio and an adjunct professor of education at the University of Dayton. He holds a doctorate of philosophy in educational administration and specializes in the application of educational and pedagogical theory in Catholic schools. Father Nuzzi has conducted many workshops across the United States and Canada to encourage the use of multiple intelligence theory in religious education. A frequent contributor to the *National Catholic Reporter*, Father Nuzzi often writes about issues of concern to Catholic school teachers and administrators.

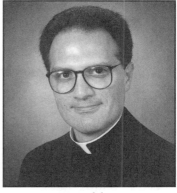

Rev. Ronald J. Nuzzi

FOREWORD

ffective teachers plan carefully, employ a broad range of learning strategies and methodically assess the extent to which students achieve desired program outcomes. They create hospitable learning environments and act on a commitment to help all students achieve. Their major focus is not whether students are learning. When students experience difficulty in class and a particular instructional approach doesn't work, teachers try another and another. Effective teachers are relentless in their persistence.

Honoring the commitment to help all learners achieve and employing a variety of instructional approaches requires an important shift in perspective for most teachers; a shift from *what and how teachers teach* to *how well students have learned*. This shift is difficult to internalize because most educators are products of a university education in which the dominant paradigm holds the teacher at the center of the learning process. Within this paradigm, students primarily experience the lecture/recitation/discussion approach to instruction.

Upon completing their professional preparation, first year teachers teach as they were taught. They employ a limited set of teaching strategies. These strategies are effective with some students and ineffective with others, and this latter fact makes it essential that they work to expand their instructional repertoire.

In this text, *Gifts of the Spirit: Multiple Intelligences in Religious Education*, Father Ron Nuzzi provides cogent, practical direction for religious educators that they might effectively teach heterogeneous groups of learners by employing a broad range of teaching/learning approaches. He does so while keeping in the forefront the importance of basing practice on sound theory.

Father Nuzzi begins with a clear explication of the essential attributes of multiple intelligence theory. He explains each of the seven types of intelligence, presents suggestions for engaging students in each intelligence area and provides sample lessons calling for the application of different intelligences at educational levels ranging from early childhood through adulthood. In addition, he offers a variety of strategies that are applicable across the curriculum.

In a particularly strong section that focuses on the Mass, Father Nuzzi presents practical ways in which teachers can initiate student involvement with multiple intelligence theory and practice. He closes with an explanation of how the celebration of the Mass calls upon the application of all types of intelligences and serves to unify multiple intelligence theory in a highly experiential way.

Teaching is a highly complex activity. In the ideal form, it is the selfless art of helping others cultivate their gifts and talents. It requires discipline and creativity as well as a commitment to continue developing different instructional approaches until each student achieves. With this work emphasizing the practical implications of multiple intelligence theory, Father Nuzzi has made a distinct contribution to the literature on teaching in general and religious education in particular.

Religious educators will find this manuscript most beneficial as they continue the challenging work of helping students internalize the message of the Gospel, become members of a supportive faith community and grow in holiness.

Joseph F. Rogus
Kuntz Professor of Education
University of Dayton

June 1996

ACKNOWLEDGEMENTS

Many events influence the development of new ideas and the application of those ideas to new situations. While my reliance on the work of Howard Gardner is clear, many others have contributed in unseen ways to the concepts presented here. Among them are

- Maureen Burke, SND, principal, Regina High School, Cleveland, Ohio, for her thoughtful review of the manuscript.

- Anne Battes Kirby, principal, Prince of Peace Catholic School in Plano, Texas, for many inspiring lessons using the theory.

- James M. Frabutt, The University of North Carolina-Greensboro, for editing and helpful revisions.

- Thomas J. Lasley, The University of Dayton, for first introducing me to Gardner's theory.

- Lars J. Lund, religion department chairperson, Junipero Serra High School, San Mateo, California, for a careful analysis of the lessons offered here.

- Lisa Ray, Loyola College, Maryland, for her research efforts.

- Joseph F. Rogus, The University of Dayton, for his steady support and encouragement.

- Mary Frances Taymans, SND and NCEA, for the invitation to pursue this topic.

- Tracy Hartzler-Toon and Cecilia Edwards of NCEA, for shepherding this manuscript through its many stages.
- Fellow teachers and catechists in Vancouver, British Columbia; Amarillo, Texas; and Seattle, Washington, who are already applying these concepts.

Many thanks to all for your generous spirit and dedicated work!

Rev. Ronald J. Nuzzi, PhD
Dayton, Ohio

May 31, 1996
Feast of the Visitation

PREFACE

"There are varieties of gifts,
but the same Spirit..."
1 Corinthians 12:4

Whenever Catholic school educators gather, there is a palpable energy arising from common interests, sense of ministry, professional commitment and shared Catholic identity. This is even more so in evidence when a particular focus shapes the agenda and conversation. Such was the case when the NCEA Secondary Schools Department sponsored a conference for Catholic high school religion teachers and campus ministers at The University of Dayton during the summer of 1995.

During this conference the patterns and possibilities defining curriculum and shaping instruction in the area of religious education were examined and explored along with the foundation for and many expressions of campus ministry. The best of pedagogy was blended with the richness of Catholic identity as expressed in classrooms and through the climate, culture and community inherent in a Catholic school. The presentations and conversation seemed too significant to end in Dayton or to be limited to a specific point in time. *Gifts of the Spirit: Multiple Intelligences in Religious Education* continues these discussions. The author, Father Ron Nuzzi, builds a bridge between the Multiple Intelligences (MI) theory and religious education at the elementary and secondary levels both in the more formal classroom setting as well as in ritual and liturgy.

MI theory may have its origin in recent history, but as is evident in this manuscript as well as in the pages of scripture; our faith and our teaching abound with expression and understanding of its meaning. Jesus the teacher and Paul the commentator draw us into the significance of many ways of learning and knowing; water, boat trips, walking and talking, fish and loaves, coins and parables long preceded the terms linguistic, musical, logical-mathematical, spatial, bodily-kinesthetic, interpersonal and intrapersonal.

So we begin with the blessing "There are varieties of gifts, but the same Spirit..."

Mary Frances Taymans, SND
Associate Executive Director
Secondary Schools Department
National Catholic Educational Association

CHAPTER I

INTRODUCTION

eachers of religious education face tremendous challenges today. Whether in the Catholic school or in the parish catechetical program, sharing the faith with the next generation of believers often presents many difficulties to even the veteran teacher. Among these challenges are: how can Gospel values be taught in persuasive and engaging ways? What is the best way to make the faith come alive for young people? What teaching techniques are best suited for study of the sacraments? Of the Scriptures? What about church history?

Adult catechists and religion teachers confront these challenges every day. While their own faith may be a deeply held, solidly grounded set of religious convictions, teaching others requires a clear, articulate presentation of the values one may have accepted a long time ago. Furthermore, while teachers have had extensive pedagogical preparation in the areas of classroom management and instructional techniques, few have received practical and professional preparation regarding the teaching of religion. In fact, few such courses exist. Teachers learn to teach religion usually by teaching religion.

In the language of teacher education, religious educators need a methods course, a "how to" discussion about teaching religion. One component of such a course would surely be Howard Gardner's theory of multiple intelligences. Gardner, a Harvard psychologist, first published his theory of an alternative view of intelligence in his 1983 book *Frames of Mind*. The response was remarkable, and soon professionals around the country began exploring ways in which the theory of multiple intelligences could be implemented. Schools soon recognized the implications of the theory for education, and gradually teachers incorporated multiple intelligences into their teaching repertoire. The theory today is a popular teaching technique that enriches classroom learning around the country.

As this booklet demonstrates, Gardner's theory has cross-curricular appeal and can be particularly helpful in religious education. In the following pages, the theory of multiple intelligences is explored and then applied to religious education. In an effort to support the teaching of religion, this booklet provides teachers with both the theoretical foundation and some concrete examples of multiple intelligence applications. While it is understood that MI theory is but one among many possible pedagogical strategies, it is an exciting approach and one that has great potential for renewing and invigorating the traditional religion class.

In a recent publication devoted to implementing MI theory in the classroom, Thomas Armstrong observed that the theory represents a philosophy of education. Armstrong's book, *Multiple Intelligences in the Classroom*, explored a variety of teaching strategies and assessment ideas that are congruent with MI theory. For the purposes of religious education, we can now explore how MI theory is congruent with many religious values and supportive of some of the basic tenets of the Christian faith.

Fundamental to Gardner's theory is the conviction, based on scientific research, that everybody possesses at least seven different intelligences, many of which have gone unnoticed. Working with a diverse population of human subjects, Gardner observed what he believed to be a biological basis for intelligence. Whether through studying the development of different abilities in children, the breakdown of mental capacities after brain damage or the intellectual prowess of exceptional populations like prodigies and savants, Gardner discerned that intelligence was a pluralistic phenomena. Some children were very gifted in art or language. Others had special talent in physical activities like sports and dance. Still others were strong in language and math. One area of strength, furthermore, did not necessarily indicate how gifted they be might be in another area. Thus, Gardner arrived at a dynamic, fluid view of intelligence.

Catholic theology has a similar point of departure, founded not on scientific study and research, but on the witness of the Scriptures and the constant tradition of the Church. Inspired by the creation accounts in the book of Genesis, Catholic teaching has clearly stated that creation is good and of God (Gen. 1:18; 21; 25; 30). A foundational text, establishing a source for human rights and human dignity can be found nearby in Genesis 1:27: "God created us in the divine image; male and female we were created." Each person has an inherent, God-given dignity. In each person resides the divine image, a divine spark, a specialness, a uniqueness that has its origin in God. It is no wonder that St. Paul claims that:

> There are different kinds of gifts, but the same spirit; there are different forms of service, but the same Lord; there are different workings but the same God who produces all of them in everyone. To each individual the manifestation of the Spirit is given for some benefit (I Cor. 12: 4-7).

Paul is suggesting that God blesses people in different ways, and while all gifts ultimately come as a grace from God, people respond to the offer of God's grace differently. Some deny them; others embrace them. Some exploit them; others develop them. But in the measure that all are possessed by a divine presence, a divine image that empowers a unique dimension of their humanity, all have some gifts to offer the human family. To each believer a unique manifestation of the divine is given for the good of the community.

Gardner may not have intended it, Scripture may not suggest it, but it is not too far a leap to build a connection between this theory of multiple intelligences and the convictions of Scripture and the Christian faith. All of us are gifted in certain ways. MI theory suggests the possible concrete manifestations of these gifts. Gardner does not appear to have been influenced by religious faith and the Bible in his scientific studies. The Scriptures certainly do not include the term *multiple intelligences*, but, the basic thrust of both of these approaches seems to be moving in the same direction. Moreover, for people of faith, Gardner's theory provides an extremely useful context for understanding, appreciating and analyzing the goodness creation.

To make clear the connections between MI theory and religious education, three topics will be discussed:

1) an overview of the theory of multiple intelligences
2) concrete examples and lesson plans for using MI theory in

religious education classes at various levels

3) multiple intelligence theory and the Mass.

Chapter II discusses the details of the theory with particular attention given to each of Gardner's seven intelligences. Appreciating the nature and manifestation of the intelligence is a necessary first step if one is eventually going to teach to the intelligence and call forth its potential.

Chapter III includes practical teaching strategies for religious education that respect the multiple intelligences. Lesson plans for a variety of subject areas in religious education and different grade levels are offered. The sample lessons give witness to resonance of MI theory with the richness of Catholic teaching.

Chapter IV explores the relationship between MI theory and the central act of Catholic life, the Eucharist. The wisdom, both of MI theory and church practice, is abundantly clear as we see in the Mass a veritable festival of the multiple intelligences.

CHAPTER II
THE THEORY OF
MULTIPLE INTELLIGENCES

ho is smartest: William Shakespeare, Albert Einstein, Pablo Picasso, Michael Jordan, Leonard Bernstein, Emily Dickenson or Martin Luther King?

- Anne Bruetsch

Schools are highly competitive places. Much of the competition in the classroom comes from a desire on the part of students to perform well academically. From the first time they are assigned homework or take a test, students learn that they will be evaluated on the basis of their work. They will receive a grade, a number or letter that measures their productivity. While educators readily affirm that these grades are not reflections of any individual's self-worth, everyone who has been a student knows the impact of receiving grades.

A good or high grade produces feelings of accomplishment and pleasure. It means that the material has been mastered, perhaps even in an excellent fashion. When students receive such evaluations, they are encouraged in their work, feel motivated to proceed and think themselves smart.

Low or failing grades can produce just the opposite reaction.

Remediation may be necessary at this point for the significant parts of the lesson have yet to be grasped. A low or failing grade communicates to the student that much has been left unlearned and it may be time to revisit the material. Such an evaluation drains a student's energy and enthusiasm and diminishes the motivation to move forward. While teachers say that a failing grade is not the end of the world, but a call to work harder, students receiving such marks often feel differently. They conclude that they are failures and not smart.

Smart. It is, perhaps, the most commonly repeated word within the walls of schools. Students with good grades are smart. Those with poor grades are not. Students with average grades are smarter than the ones with poor grades, and the top-notch, straight-A students are the smartest of all. To a certain extent, schools function as a way to sort and separate varying degrees of smartness among students. Grades, tests, awards, class ranks, grade point averages and standardized tests all serve as ways to determine how smart students are.

How You Are Smart vs. How Smart You Are

The theory of multiple intelligences challenges this view of *smart* as being a single and isolated measure of a student's intelligence. MI theory suggests that educational efforts measuring student intelligence may be misdirected. In short, schools should not be investing energy in evaluating how smart students are, but in helping students discern how they are smart.

Questioning the traditional measure of intelligence and the single IQ score, Gardner sought in *Frames of Mind* to study human cognitive development in a broader way. Proceeding from the conviction that intelligence is observed to be contextual, Gardner refashioned the definition of intelligence. His studies revealed a group of at least seven intelligences under which the wide spectrum of human potential and giftedness could be understood. Schools and society had come to characterize intelligence much too simply, Gardner believed, and as a result of an extended observation and study, he offered a new view of intelligence.

For Gardner, intelligence includes at least three characteristics:
- the ability to solve problems
- the ability to pose new problems
- the ability to fashion a product or provide a service which is

valued in one or more cultural settings.

This description of intelligence is provocative more for what it does not say than for what it says. The new description is not focused on measurement or on attempts to quantify intelligence. It does not address the classic question of nature versus nurture, i.e., whether intelligence is natural and inborn or learned and acquired through practice. It does direct our attention to a specific cultural context, leading to the inevitable conclusion that whatever intelligence is, it is first of all, highly contextual.

Everyday human experiences provide credible proof of this claim. Think of the young child, struggling with music lessons, but remarkably adept with the latest video game. The notes on the scale seem confusing, but hand-eye coordination comes with ease. There is the fifth grader who moves somewhat awkwardly and is often embarrassed in physical education class. Yet, in the classroom this individual demonstrates a talent with mathematical calculations equal to a high school junior. A high school student cannot make heads or tails out of geography, but is fluent in several languages, due in large part to a multicultural early childhood.

Adults are no different. Some adults can disassemble just about anything in an effort to repair or understand its functioning. Others are immensely challenged by the turning of a simple screw. With a set of directions and a map, some drivers can find their way around unfamiliar territory without difficulty. Others get lost or distracted a few miles from home. While everyone has met the highly verbal chatter-box who just loves to talk, socialize, and be the life of the party, we know, too, that others prefer quiet, solitude, and their own company over that of other people. The talker is accustomed to articulate, verbal persuasion and thinks nothing of arguing about a traffic violation. The introspective individual, completely shaken by the experience of being pulled over, just wants to get it over with as soon as possible.

Intelligence, understood as the ability to solve and create problems or the ability to fashion valued products, is contextual. It goes far beyond what might ordinarily be accepted in school as smart. It involves a range of human experiences, situations, and real life problems that are encountered in life every day.

Are You Smart?

According to the theory of multiple intelligences, every person is smart and has ability in at least seven different areas. All of the varying types and degrees of giftedness and intelligence that we observe in school and in normal, daily living can be categorized under one or more of seven intelligences. The seven kinds of smart or the seven types of intelligence are:

- linguistic intelligence or word smart
- musical intelligence or music smart
- logical-mathematical intelligence or number smart
- spatial intelligence or picture smart
- bodily-kinesthetic intelligence or body smart
- interpersonal intelligence or people smart
- intrapersonal intelligence or self smart.

These seven intelligences can be further classified according to their relationship to the learning environment. Thus, the seven intelligences can be understood as language-related, object-related and person-related.

Language-related	Object-related	Person-related
linguistic	logical-mathematical	interpersonal
musical	spatial	intrapersonal
	bodily-kinesthetic	

Language-related intelligence, including verbal and musical skill, engage both auditory and oral functions. Gardner was convinced that these functions were central to the development of verbal and rhythmic skill. In fact, Gardner hypothesized that back in some uncharted area of evolution, music and language must have arisen from the same early attempts at communication and self-expression.

Object-related intelligences are stimulated and engaged by concrete objects and experiences one encounters in the environment. Such objects may include the physical structure of the environment itself, concrete things that are found in the environment and abstractions, like numbers, used to organize the environment.

Person-related intelligences engage the sense of self and the relationship of the self to other persons. They include the often competing and simultaneous interests of coming to know oneself as an individual and discovering one's community.

The Seven Intelligences

It is important to remember that Gardner claimed that every person possesses all seven intelligences to some degree. In fact, part of what constitutes the uniqueness of each person may be understood as a particular mix of the intelligences present in any individual. If this is true, then the task of education becomes fashioning instruction in such a way that it respects the seven intelligences. It means taking care to teach to the different intelligences, discover students' strengths and weaknesses and address their different learning styles. By nurturing those intelligences that are strong and developing those that are not as strong, teachers can facilitate a healthy integration of the seven intelligences in their students.

A brief look at each individual intelligence will foster an understanding of the unique properties it manifests. Such an understanding will also facilitate planning to teach to specific intelligences.

LINGUISTIC

Linguistic Intelligence

Linguistic intelligence is the ability to use words and language effectively. It is manifested in both oral and written form. Gardner believed that poetry represented a prime example of linguistic intelligence (*Frames of Mind*, 73). Persuasive speakers, lawyers, politicians, homilists and salespeople have this intelligence and use it to communicate their ideas forcefully and with clarity. Writers and poets exhibit linguistic intelligence as well and call upon it often to craft a particularly clever phrase, imaginative metaphor or creative thought.

Gardner claimed that at least four aspects of linguistic intelligence have proven themselves important in today's society (*Frames of Mind*, 78):

1) the rhetorical aspect of language—the ability to use language to convince others of a course of action
2) the mnemonic potential of language—the ability to use language to help in recalling information
3) the ability to use language to explain—a critical requirement in educational processes
4) the ability to use language to explain language—another key component of the educational setting.

Armstrong called this intelligence *word smart* because of its intrinsic relationship to words and language (*7 Kinds of Smart*, 9). Word smart is a helpful way to think about this intelligence for it often manifests itself as a strong interest in the spoken or printed word. Individuals with linguistic intelligence love to read, tell jokes, make plays on words or puns, write letters and develop slogans and sayings.

Because of its strong emphasis on lectures, written assignments, reading and textbooks, schools have traditionally had a clear interest in linguistic intelligence. Gardner maintained that this focus on linguistic intelligence often means that other intelligences are ignored or forgotten.

Musical Intelligence

MUSICAL

Musical intelligence is the ability to perceive and express variations in rhythm, pitch and melody. It includes the ability to compose music as well the capacity to appreciate music and to distinguish subtleties in its form. Individuals with musical intelligence often turn to writing music and composing as a vehicle for self-expression. Some of the greatest pieces of classical music, contemporary country music and Rock-and-Roll Hall-of-Fame pieces come from those who were gifted in the area.

But musical intelligence goes beyond the ability to compose. A person with musical intelligence has an ear for tunes. This is the person who is always humming some melody or who cannot stop singing the last song heard. Singing in the shower, singing along with the car radio while driving, tapping along to the beat—all these are signs of musical intelligence.

Schools have regularly addressed musical intelligence as a talent or special gift only for the musician or choir member. It has been common place for music classes to be the first cut or dropped for a special schedule or curriculum reduction. Unfortunately, musical education has been seen as a curricular extra, a nice course if there is time and money, but expendable if courses must be limited. Many theorists today believe that music is an appropriate vehicle to teach a variety of skills that are readily transferable to learning in any area. Because of music's dependence on special ratios, proportions and recurring patterns, Gardner observed that mathematics has an intrinsic relationship to music.

One does not have to look far to observe the influence that music has on today's young people. The ubiquitous walkman; large, portable stereo systems; the popularity of concerts and music groups; and 24-hour-a-day MTV all testify to the broad of appeal of music to modern culture. Because schools have been myopic in their treatment of musical intelligence, this is a particularly fertile area for educators to mine.

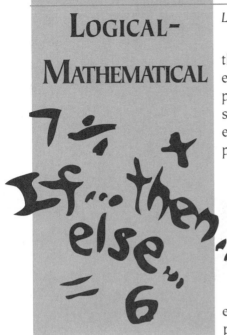

LOGICAL-
MATHEMATICAL

Logical-Mathematical Intelligence

Logical-mathematical intelligence is the ability to use numbers correctly and effectively and to use reason to solve problems. This intelligence is readily observed in one's ability to solve mathematical calculations of increasing complexity and capacity to generate categories and classifications. The person with logical-mathematical intelligence easily perceives patterns and can follow complex series of commands.

Logical-mathematical intelligence is a highly prized ability in our culture. Bankers, mathematicians, scientists of all types, statisticians, computer technicians, engineers, architects and tax collectors are all people with logical-mathematical intelligence. Calculating the anticipated total price of your groceries requires logical-mathematical intelligence, as does dividing the miles to the beach or ski slopes by the speed you are driving to determine how much longer you will be on the road.

Scientific reasoning and the scientific method are properly understood as being manifestations of logical-mathematical reasoning. Such reasoning would include the ability to conduct experiments, create and test competing hypotheses and make predictions based on observed patterns. Exercising a *process of elimination* is an example of logical-mathematical intelligence at work.

Because society places a high value on logical-mathematical dexterity, schools have traditionally emphasized these skills. Science and math scores are often the first standards used to evaluate academic achievement or to compare one group of students' learning to another. Logical-mathematical ability has come to be seen as a prerequisite for advanced work or study in nearly all fields of science.

Spatial Intelligence

Spatial intelligence is the ability to perceive the physical world clearly and be able to think in images, pictures and mental illustrations. People with spatial intelligence are highly visual learners, requiring to see and experience a phenomenon before it can be adequately understood. Gardner believed that spatial intelligence manifests itself in at least three ways:

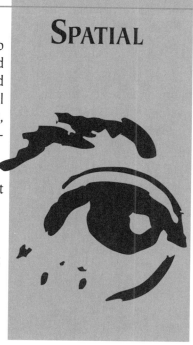

SPATIAL

- the ability to perceive things accurately
- the ability to maneuver an object through space by imagining it rotated or by seeing it from various perspectives
- the ability to represent one's ideas in a two or three dimensional form

It should be noted that while spatial intelligence has a strong visual component, it is not synonymous with accurate vision. The visual component of spatial intelligence refers more directly to the ability to visualize in one's mind and create mental representations of reality. Thus, a blind person may have keen spatial intelligence.

Individuals with spatial intelligence are very observant of shapes, colors, lines, the use of space and relationships between objects. They have a strong sense of geographical orientation and can easily orient themselves in unfamiliar surroundings. They read maps well and follow directions without problem. Even in a new environment, such as a large, sprawling amusement park, they quickly learn their way around and provide directions to assist others. They remember where the car is parked and have a certain passion about things being in their proper places, for it is by visualizing the proper place that they find the things they seek.

Spatial intelligence is required for such occupations as artists, pilots, professional drivers, tour guides, architects, interior designers and contractors. Hunters use spatial intelligence; so do the Girl Scouts and Boy Scouts. Photography involves an appreciation and expression of spatial intelligence as well.

Schools have not been especially strong or interested in teaching spatial intelligence. While spatial thinking is directly connected to the visual arts, artistic expression is usually not taught with the same rigor and dedication as other subjects. Indeed, as we have observed in the case of music, art is often the very first class cast aside, skipped or even ignored. This lack of interest in art as a true expression of an intelligence is also betrayed by our vocabulary. Art is not a *class*, but an activity. We do not have Art class, we have an art activity. Math is class. English is class. Art is something else.

Bodily-Kinesthetic Intelligence

BODILY-KINESTHETIC

Bodily-kinesthetic intelligence is the ability to use our bodies to express ideas and feelings and to perform certain valuable functions, as well the capacity to manipulate and handle objects skillfully. As the name indicates, this intelligence really addresses two related abilities: the ability to exercise a certain degree of control over our body movements and a facility in using one's hands to shape, transform, produce or create things. Since we are sensory beings, bodily-kinesthetic intelligence concerns the avenue through which we come to know and experience all of reality. We do not simply have bodies; we are our bodies.

This intelligence is evident in many valued settings today. The professional athlete must have it. The dancer, sculptor, painter and mime possess it as well. Surgeons work on developing and strengthening this intelligence. Mechanics and builders must also have a well developed bodily-kinesthetic intelligence.

Individuals manifest their bodily-kinesthetic intelligence through their chosen leisure activities. Running, racquetball, horse-back riding, basketball, swimming, walking and hiking are all examples of bodily-kinesthetic energy at work. Since everything that happens to us in some way must happen to our bodies, we engage this intelligence constantly.

Society in general has become very health and body conscious in recent years. Exercise programs, health spas and diet workshops all attest to the increasing interest in developing and caring for our bodies. This interest is present in schools especially in physical education programs that now focus on developing life-long interests and activities, rather than on recreational interests. Intramural sports teams, organized more for cooperation than competition, encourage players of varying ability to participate in physical activity without the concern for winning that drives interscholastic events. Bodily-kinesthetic development is, however, far too often confined to the playing field or gymnasium.

INTERPERSONAL

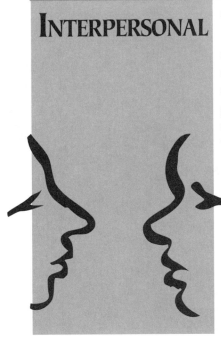

Interpersonal Intelligence

Interpersonal intelligence is the skill of understanding, perceiving and appreciating the feelings and moods of others. It manifests itself in the ability to get along well with others, work cooperatively and communicate effectively. The individual with interpersonal intelligence can see things from the perspective of others. With this understanding of the alternative perspective, such individuals are often able to motivate others to do certain things.

Gardner believed that interpersonal intelligence included the ability to persuade or influence others. The ability to see things as others see them gives the leader, for example, an uncanny advantage in addressing the concerns of the opposition. For this reason, interpersonal intelligence may be found in a compassionate, selfless, altruistic person who, sensing the needs of others, moves to meet them immediately. A more self-centered person with interpersonal intelligence might use the same ability to discern the fear of the community in an effort to control the group for sinister purposes. History is replete with both types of leaders.

Students learn a great deal about interpersonal intelligence through the normal process of socialization that occurs when they first arrive at school. Learning to interpret and respond to facial expressions, voice, gestures and other signals all point to a growing interpersonal intelligence. Group projects or tasks that require collaboration also draw out interpersonal skills.

While some interpersonal intelligence is required of everyone, it is particularly important for those who would lead others or be charged with the care of others. Administrators, supervisors and politicians need this skill in order to understand and respond to the needs of their respective constituencies. Physicians are often praised or criticized for having developed or ignored this intelligence in relationship to their medical expertise. Interpersonal intelligence is thus a part of every social interaction. And as we can see from the above examples, it has more to do with being able to sense the feelings and needs of others than it does with being highly verbal and articulate. While interpersonal intelligence may be a part of the personality profile of the incessant talker, its essence lies in attentiveness to others, not self.

INTRAPERSONAL

Intrapersonal Intelligence

Intrapersonal intelligence is best described as self-knowledge. "To thy own self be true," the advice of Socrates, expresses the core of this intelligence. Intrapersonal intelligence is the ability to understand one's own self, perceive accurately one's strengths and weaknesses and draw on this understanding as a means to direct one's actions. It is a type of introspective focus that directs its attention to self-analysis and self-understanding.

Intrapersonal intelligence manifests itself in the desire to be alone to sort things out, the need for quiet and free time and the desire to meditate or reflect. People strong in this intelligence are often deep thinkers and can occupy themselves for long periods of time with their own thoughts and questions. Gardner believed that intrapersonal intelligence was directly related to interpersonal intelligence in that the ability to reach out effectively to others is rooted in knowing oneself first.

This is not an intelligence that has been addressed in the traditional curriculum found in schools. With all the noise and distractions of modern life, there hardly seems an appropriate place to encourage people to be quiet, get in touch with themselves and reflect silently. Yet, if Gardner is correct, developing this quiet, contemplative sense of self is a necessary step in the process of socialization. Too often we spend our time fleeing silence or solitude. Has anyone been taught to be still? Not simply as a disciplinary exercise—quiet for the sake of order—but silence for the sake of listening to one's innermost self?

Individuals with high intrapersonal intelligence may be perceived as loners or as excessively individualistic. They may prefer to work on their own rather than in a group, or feel the need to sort things out on their own before being comfortable contributing to the group. As we will see, this intelligence is a particularly fertile area to develop a religious sensibility. By relating intrapersonal dynamics to prayer and a religious tradition, intrapersonal intelligence can been seen as a vehicle for spiritual reflection.

Chapter III

The Multiple

Intelligences in

Religious Education

I n the first decade of its existence, multiple intelligence theory has come to be a widely recognized approach to teaching. While a few schools have adopted MI theory as the governing educational philosophy of the entire curriculum, most teachers use MI theory and practice as one way among many to enrich and diversify their classroom teaching. Seen as a valuable addition to a teacher's repertoire of classroom approaches, MI theory has the potential to bring new life and new energy to classrooms.

A variety of resources exist to assist teachers in planning lessons that respect and nurture the multiple intelligences. Some claim the MI thinking is really a mind-set, and that once developed, a teacher can learn to think in terms of the various multiple intelligences. This section is an effort to stimulate the thinking of religion teachers in the area of multiple intelligences. Given Gardner's theory and the fluid view of intelligence he has proposed, what might MI theory have to contribute to religious education? Were we to assume an MI context, what might our religious education classes look like?

Linguistic Intelligence

Oral expression is the currency of most classrooms. Whether voiced by the teacher or student, verbal exchanges constitute much of what happens in school. Ideas for developing linguistic intelligence in religious education include:

—*Etymology of religious terms.* Have students research the origin and root of new terms. The Latin or Greek root of many words is instructive and carries a meaning not always commonly known. The word "eucharist," meaning *to give thanks,* is a good example. Many names from the Bible also carry a deeper meaning that relate to circumstances in the individual's life. For example, the name Isaac is related to the Hebrew word for laughter because Abraham laughs at God when he is told he will have a son in his old age. The name of the famous archangel Michael is actually a Hebrew question, "who is like God?" Michael has the job of challenging those who would claim to rival God, and his name itself is thus a blunt rebuke.

—*Word games and puzzles.* A variety of software is available today that generates crosswords puzzles and other word games based on vocabulary selected by the teacher. A self-developed classroom version of Trivial Pursuit based on sacraments, church history, the Bible or the lives of the saints would also be an engaging possibility. A school-house version of the popular television show "Wheel of Fortune," where students guess a word or term based on viewing only a few letters, would call forth linguistic intelligence.

—*Respecting books, starting with the Bible.* Instilling in students a love of reading and a concomitant respect for books are essential if a school goal is to develop a lifelong love of learning. Having a place of honor to enthrone the Bible is a step in this direction. Were every grade and class to develop rituals around the Bible, students would learn repeatedly by example that God's word is to be respected. Drawing students' attention to other important books or having them available and on display is another way to highlight the importance of written traditions. Many Catholic schools, named after a saint, feast or church leader, can have books by or about their namesake readily available and accessible to students.

—*Storytelling.* Often viewed as entertainment in the elementary classroom or library, storytelling is a potent teaching tool and its power should not be underestimated. Families depend on stories to teach children about their history. Nearly all cultures have some system, often highly developed, for articulating and passing on the common cultural heritage of the community. Stories educate, and the images they instill remain with people for a lifetime.

The Scriptures are, of course, our first and best source of the great stories of our faith. Other sources include the lives of the saints, the struggles of people known through the news or current events, examples from our own lives as teachers and examples selected from the shared history of the school. Many preachers know from experience that some of their best crafted material, theologically astute and cleverly delivered, is forgotten before Mass is over. But the heartfelt story is recounted again and again; its message and power remain strong.

—*Emphasize writing and speaking skills.* Teachers devote much time and energy to these skills already as they are prized in nearly every school. Religious education can make use of these skills in such things as memorizing important prayers or Scripture passages, tape recording the recitations of them and having students keep a personal journal where they write about what they learned or felt in class.

Musical and rhythmic intelligences are vital to religious education because of their power to touch the soul. As Saint Augustine remarked centuries ago, "those who sing, pray twice." Furthermore, there is a vibrant and rich tradition in the church of sacred song and chant. Music and congregational singing are an integral part of every worship experience, or at least should be. Ideas for nurturing musical intelligence include:

—*A class song, school song or alma mater.* High schools typically have a song that was written to be an expression of the school spirit, but many elementary schools do not. Such songs have a unique power to tap into the emotional side of school life, especially if they are sung regularly and with reverence. In the absence of a school song, a class song is a viable option. In schools where the song is really working as an expression and celebration of the community's life of faith, it can become the vehicle for bonding the school community and for initiating newcomers to the fold. The school song functions much as a theme song for the life that is shared. Notice that every television show has such a theme song and that students can sing just about any one of them.

The song can be sung as the first and last corporate act of every school year. It can be sung to individuals on special occasions as a sign of support, welcome or farewell. And, if crafted to include the religious and faith dimension of the school, it can be sung to God as a prayer.

—*The liturgical hymns and responses for the Mass.* There is no reason why students cannot be taught a variety of musical settings for the responses sung at Mass. This would include more than brief music practice before Mass, but a comprehensive effort to teach the entire community different renditions of the *Gloria; Holy, Holy, Holy; Memorial Acclamation; The Great Amen;* and *The Lamb of God.* All staff and faculty should be involved as well as it is the whole school community who celebrates at Mass.

—*Song as prayer.* It is common, if not universal, that daily life begins in the Catholic school with a prayer. Many schools even begin each class with a prayer, led by a student or the teacher. Prayer in this context, however, usually means somebody speaking a prayer. Why not a song? Why not a song as the day's end? Everyone is disposed at the end of the day for a little joy. A dismissal song might be just the ticket to capture that spirit and offer it to God as the school's prayer.

—*Background and mood music.* Certain lessons suggest the addition of background or mood music to emphasize the content being taught. Flowing water might be played as baptism is discussed, trumpets during a study of Easter. Some teachers have successfully integrated classical music into their classrooms as a way of relaxing students and reducing stress. Appropriate musical selections could also be used to excite and energize students, focus their attention or encourage their working together. Songs or melodies associated with repeated activities encourage student cooperation and create a musical expectation for accomplishing certain tasks. For example, a unique melody to signal the beginning of religion class, another verse to indicate that Bibles should be distributed, and another song to prepare for Mass help to organize classroom activities in a way that invites students to cooperate.

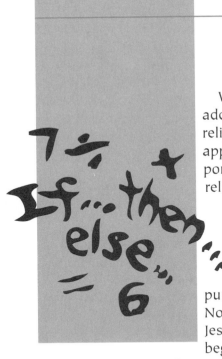

LOGICAL-MATHEMATICAL INTELLIGENCE

While this intelligence is traditionally addressed with great interest in schools, religious educators may see little of value to apply to the religion class. Ways to incorporate logical-mathematical intelligence in religious education include:

—*Indicating the religious significance of certain numbers.* The number 40, for example, is associated with purification and preparedness. Hence, the Israelites wander in the desert for 40 years in pursuit of the Promised Land. It rains on Noah and the ark for 40 days and 40 nights. Jesus fasts in the desert for 40 days before beginning his ministry. There are 40 days in Lent, and 40 days between Easter and Ascension.

Similar exercises can be used to teach about other events, beliefs and stories and their relationship to certain numbers. The number seven is associated with perfection, the number three with the Trinity, the number 12 with the Apostles and the tribes of ancient Israel.

—*Create math problems and number games with religion material.* What is numerical in religion? Plenty. How many are there in each category below:

- sacraments?
- commandments?
- apostles?
- prophets?
- miracles of Jesus?

- testaments in the Bible?
- books in the Old Testament?
- letters of St. Paul?
- journeys of St. Paul?
- people at the foot of the cross?

Older students could be encouraged to calculate the length of certain journeys mentioned in the Bible and approximate the time it would take to complete such a journey. Comparing the length of different texts is also a way to engage this intelligence. Which is longer, the Gospel of Mark or a Sunday Mass?

—*Activities in celebration of holidays, Sundays and holy days.* Most experienced teachers have a collection of resources for teaching and celebrating various special events throughout the year. There are special art activities associated with Halloween, others for Thanksgiving and different rites to welcome Spring in the classroom. The same can be accomplished in relation to religious events so that students come to associate special feasts and holidays with activities that they enjoy. The liturgical seasons of Lent and Advent are especially good times for such activities.

There is no need for teachers to feel that new and increasingly clever ideas must be generated each year. The habit of repeating a particularly engaging activity year after year in a school is just the reinforcement needed to carry that practice over into adult life. The same is true for activities repeated in the classroom over the years by an individual teacher. Younger siblings often look forward to be involved in the project or activity they heard about or observed from a distance. In such cases, the continuity of the experience and the repetition of the activity is more educational than any new idea could ever be.

One Catholic elementary school in the Midwest decided on this Advent activity: On the first day of each week of Advent they were in school, the day began with a school-wide assembly and prayer service in the gymnasium. The prayer services began in darkness. The lights were not turned on, the shades were drawn over the windows. Instead of lighting the traditional wreath, different grades were assigned to bring flashlights to the prayer service. Each week, more and more students and staff showed up with flashlights so that by Advent's end, the light in the gym was becoming increasingly bright. One cannot but imagine that these students heard Isaiah's prophecy with a new urgency on Christmas Eve: "The people who walked in darkness have seen a great light" (Isaiah 9:1).

SPATIAL INTELLIGENCE

Spatial intelligence is perhaps best utilized in religious education when it involves imagination activities requiring visualization. Other techniques can address the more concrete dimensions of spatial intelligence. Some possible approaches in religious education include:

— *Jumping into biblical situations.* Have students imagine that they are part of the story. What is happening? What does it look like? How might they have responded to the situation? To Jesus? To Moses? A variation of this activity is to have students create a story to supplement or to complete an episode that is not fully disclosed in Scripture. *The Fourth Wise Man* is an example of this approach. Ask students to tell you about the innkeeper at Christmas who has no room for Mary and Joseph. How about the bad thief? The carpenter who made Jesus' cross? None of these are described in any detail in the Bible, but posing the question engages the imagination and brings the story to life in a new way.

—*Maps and models.* The use of maps and scale models helps students to understand what they are being taught in a very concrete way. While some might argue that such efforts take away the need for visualization, the thinking required to interpret a map or create a scale model is a higher order skill. Drawing sketches or diagrams also engages similar skills. Such techniques can be applied to teach ideas about church architecture, the geography of the Holy Land, the structure of the temple in Jerusalem, the arrangement at the Last Supper, the walls of Jericho, the waters of the River Jordan or the history of Christianity.

—*Graphic organizers.* Visual displays in the classroom that summarize an entire content area or organize the details of an instructional unit reinforce learning by tapping into this intelligence. A timeline displaying the history of church, including important events and significant people, creates an overall context into which each lesson can fit. Posters about the seven sacraments serve the same purpose. Teacher-made charts outlining prominent groups such as prophets, evangelists, apostles, martyrs and popes helps to situate new information in this general framework.

—*Graphics software and Hypercard applications.* Computers may have found their way into Catholic schools and Catholic classrooms, but religious education has yet to find much use for technology. Graphic software is very popular among children and young people for it allows them to draw, color and create images with ease. Students can be encouraged to use such software to express elements of the lesson, create original designs and draw or sketch what they are being taught. *Hypercard,* a type of computer software, can be used by the teacher to create a multimedia presentation or by advanced students to create a visual report rather than a written one.

BODILY-KINESTHETIC INTELLIGENCE

Using our bodies to express what is in our minds is not an entirely new concept in religious education. Activities that promote bodily-kinesthetic intelligence have long had a place in Religion class. Some common activities include:

—Gestures to accompany songs and prayers. Teaching students expressive body movements to accompany the Lord's Prayer or a liturgical hymn is an excellent way to incorporate a bodily-kinesthetic dimension in religious education. Teachers may want to consider having older students work together to design such movements and then teach them to younger students.

—Use of drama in the classroom. Acting out important stories or biblical events and letting students role play is a good way to get a large group of students involved and focused on an activity. As the teacher reads a passage, the whole class can use body movements to interpret what is going on in the story. In a more formal approach, the teacher may prepare and assign parts to different students.

—Religious crafts. The opportunity to reinforce religious lessons should not be lost during art or crafts time. Craft activities where students construct things can be oriented to the content of a recent Religion lesson.

—Dance. Many schools have experimented with dance in a liturgical context, for example, as the bread and wine are offered at Mass or as an after communion prayer of thanksgiving. These dances have most often been performed by one student or several as the majority observed. Large group dances, where everyone is involved, provides a more complete experience and diminishes the sense of individual performance that often accompanies solo dances. Anyone who has attended a wedding reception and witnessed the crowd cheer as a favorite melody knows how powerful the large group dance can be.

The movements need not be complex or original. Often enough the beauty of the dance is in its repetition of simple forms. A popular circle dance, with movements for a large group, is done to the Quaker hymn, "Simple Gifts."

—*Everyday use of ritual gestures.* Catholic practice is filled with gestures and movements that are intended to express an inner disposition toward God or toward others. These include genuflection, the sign of the cross, blessing the senses, bowing, kneeling, the sign of peace, the laying on of hands and any number of combinations of these. In Mexico, parents traditionally bless their children when they leave home for a special event or any period of time. Other cultures bow as a sign of respect for each other and for the image of God present in others. Any number of these religious gestures could be used in the classroom. In preparation for certain events, students could be encouraged to pray for each other and sign each other's senses with the sign of the cross. Teachers could pray for their class as they departed for vacation and bless each of the students as they leave. A ritual bow or exchange of a sign of peace might be a good way to begin the lunch break or even end the day.

INTERPERSONAL INTELLIGENCE

Interpersonal intelligence, or *people smart*, is the ability to discern and interpret the feelings, moods and intentions of others, and then to relate to them in an appropriate fashion based on that knowledge. Manifested in the ability to get along with others, to work and play together and in motivating others, interpersonal intelligence contains a very Christian component of living peaceably with one's neighbors. Approaches to focus on interpersonal skills in religious education include:

—*Cooperative learning.* As a pedagogical style, cooperative learning is implicitly Christian. Based more on group processes than individual ones, cooperative learning turns attention to the progress of the group and away from the isolated performance of individuals. With its insistence on group rewards but with individual accountability, cooperative learning lends itself to teaching a variety of pro-social, Christian behaviors. Any lesson or a part of any unit can be taught using this method.

—*Peer tutoring and peer sharing.* The simplest way to implement peer work is by asking students to turn to one other student and share on a specific topic. It might be at the beginning of a lesson or a new unit. In such a case, students could be invited to explore what they already know about marriage. Another possibility is to pause after presenting new information and ask students to turn to each other and summarize or repeat what they just heard. This is a particularly effective strategy when the new material is somewhat complicated. "Explain to each other what you understand to be the difference between Protestant and Catholic Bibles." A good way to generate questions about a topic, beyond asking the entire class "are there any questions?", is to instruct students to share one question with each other about the lesson.

—*Teaching other students.* Experienced teachers know the challenge of learning new material and then attempting to teach it to others. There are those who claim that you never really understand a subject unless you are able to teach it to others. While we may acquire new ideas, thoughts and information in matters of religious education, it can be argued that we do not readily appropriate that material until we have articulated it for another. Thus, when eighth graders complete their preparation for the sacrament of Confirmation, would not their understanding and appreciation of the sacrament grow were they to plan and execute a lesson on the Holy Spirit for a class from a lower grade? Could Senior Religion include teaching a lesson to first year students on community as the newcomers begin a study of Eucharist?

—*Games and simulations*. Games are activities that students readily approach with enthusiasm and interest. Besides engaging a variety of skills, board games focused on religious education can be used as an exciting teaching tool. Religious versions of *Trivial Pursuit* or other popular games that can be adapted to religious education provide a fun way for students to learn. Simulations engage a certain degree of creativity in asking students to imagine a different setting or to behave as if they were someone else. Simulations can be helpful activities after reading about another historical period or learning about customs that seem out of place in today's society.

INTRAPERSONAL INTELLIGENCE

Intrapersonal intelligence, often neglected in wider society, should occupy a prominent place in religious education. Intrapersonal intelligence can be encouraged in religious education in any of the following ways:

—*Quiet time for prayer.* Students can be taught the importance of silence and the long-standing faith tradition that God speaks to us in the silence of our hearts. These quiet times for introspection and thinking can be brief or they can be more developed, as in a guided imagery prayer.

—*Journal writing.* Students can keep a special journal where they write about their thoughts, feelings and reactions in relation to religion class. This can be especially helpful when difficult or controversial areas are being addressed, such as hunger, poverty, violence and ethical issues. The journal can be a place where students are encouraged to get in touch with their own feelings.

—*Personal prayer writing.* At the beginning of the year or at the start of a new unit, students can be guided in writing their own personal prayer. These prayers can be of a general nature or based on the specific needs and goals that students may have. At appropriate times, the prayers can be offered. This also gives teachers a chance to pray for their students, and if the teachers participate as well and write a prayer, their students also have a way of praying for them. This activity can be expanded to include a class prayer for those who are sick or absent, who are travelling or who we know to be undergoing a difficult struggle.

—*Autobiographical connections.* Religious education takes root the best when it is connected to real life experiences and our personal histories. It is one thing to teach about marriage and quite another to speak from the experience of being married. If students are encouraged to relate what they are learning to their own lives and experiences, a deeper understanding will result. For example, instruction on Jesus healing the sick could include asking students to think about a time when they were sick. Teaching about the commandments might include asking students to recall one time when they hurt someone by fighting, not telling the whole truth or not following direction.

—*Self-assessment exercises.* The traditional examination of conscience before a sacramental confession is an exercise of intrapersonal intelligence. Expanding on this concept, students can be invited to complete self-assessments frequently in keeping with the content of religion class. Questions organizing such reflection may include: "what mistakes did I make?", "where did I do well?", "what do I need to study again?".

SAMPLE RELIGIOUS EDUCATION LESSONS
USING THE MULTIPLE INTELLIGENCES

The following examples of religious education lessons are inspired by multiple intelligence theory. They are designed for different grade levels in an attempt to demonstrate some possible avenues for implementing MI practices in the teaching of religion. The lessons are easily adaptable to other situations and catechetical environments.

RELIGION CLASS #1

Grade Level: Preschool
Topic: The cross
Objective: To teach students to recognize a cross.

Students will see and experience different kinds of crosses (parenthetical remarks indicate the intelligence involved).

- Have the teacher display a cross and explain what a cross is. (linguistic)

- Have students make crosses with their bodies. (bodily-kinesthetic, intrapersonal)

- Encourage students to make crosses with their bodies in small groups, then as one large group. (interpersonal, bodily-kinesthetic)

- Look for crosses in the classroom. (spatial)

- Compare the shapes and sizes of different crosses. (logical-mathematical)

- Sing a song about crosses or about Jesus' cross. (musical)

- Read a selection from the Gospel about Jesus' cross. (linguistic)

RELIGION CLASS #2

Grade Level: 1st grade
Topic: Reading the Bible
Objective: To help students develop a respect for the Bible.

Students will experience different ways of discovering what is in the Bible.

- Teacher reads a story from the Bible. (linguistic)

- Play a video or cartoon animation of a Bible story. (spatial)

- Sing a song based on a Bible story. (musical)

- Dramatize the story with students acting it out. (bodily-kinesthetic, interpersonal)

- Compare some Bibles to other books in the classroom. (logical-mathematical)

- Have students study a Bible to learn three things about it. (intrapersonal)

RELIGION CLASS #3

Grade Level: Primary
Topic: Cooperation & respect
Objective: To help students develop skills in working together.

Students will work, talk and play together in order to complete assigned tasks.

- Have the class work in pairs, and give each pair materials to draw and color a picture together. (interpersonal, spacial)

- Make a puzzle out of each picture by cutting with a scissors. (spatial, interpersonal, bodily-kinesthetic)

- Have each pair exchange their puzzle with another pair and put them together. (interpersonal, intrapersonal, spatial)

- Mix the pieces from the two puzzles and have each pair sort them out. (logical-mathematical)

- Ask students to talk about what was difficult and what was easy in working together. (intrapersonal, linguistic)

- Learn a song about cooperation or the virtues of working together. (musical)

- Read a story about children who do not get along and ask students to think of ways to make the story better. (linguistic, intrapersonal)

RELIGION CLASS #4

Grade Level: Intermediate
Topic: Creation
Objective: To learn about the seven days of creation from the Book of Genesis.

Students will understand that all of creation is good and comes from God.

- Ask the class to discuss from where everything on earth came. (interpersonal, logical-mathematical, linguistic)

- Listen to a tape recording of a reading of each day of creation. (linguistic)

- Have students draw or sketch the events of each day of creation. (spatial, logical-mathematical)

- Dramatize the day of creation where God creates human beings. (bodily-kinesthetic)

- Using the melody of "The Twelve Days of Christmas," create a song about the seven days of creation. (musical)

- Watch the creation segment of the film, "The Ten Commandments." (spatial)

- Read the creation story from the Book of Genesis as part of a concluding prayer on this lesson. (linguistic, intrapersonal)

RELIGION CLASS #5

Grade Level: Intermediate
Topic: The Ten Commandments
Objective: To introduce students to the Ten Commandments

Students will be able to express an understanding of each of the Ten Commandments.

- Have a graphic organizer, poster or bulletin board that depicts the Ten Commandments. (spatial)

- Ask students to write and copy the Ten Commandments from the display. (linguistic)

- Write each commandment on a separate card and number it; mix up the cards and have students identify each commandment. (logical-mathematical)

- Have the students form the numbers one through ten with their bodies as each commandment is discussed. (bodily-kinesthetic)

- Ask students to create a hand gesture or sign language for a commandment of particular interest. (bodily-kinesthetic)

- Ask students which commandments they think are the hardest to follow. (intrapersonal, interpersonal)

- Have the students brainstorm ideas to state each commandment positively, as something good to do, rather than some action to avoid. (logical-mathematical, linguistic)

- Use a series of musical notes, rather than numbers, to indicate each commandment. (musical)

RELIGION CLASS #6

Grade Level: Junior High
Topic: Saint Francis of Assisi
Objective: To study the life and work of Saint Francis of Assisi

Students will be able to express an understanding of the teachings of Saint Francis of Assisi through a study of his life.

- Learn and play a song about Saint Francis such as *Brother Sun and Sister Moon* or *Make Me a Channel of Your Peace*. (musical)

- Locate Assisi on a map of Italy. (spatial)

- Read selections from different biographies of Saint Francis, such as Butler's *Lives of the Saints* or Murray Bodo's *The Song of the Sparrow*. (linguistic)

- Have students work in groups with the biographical reading and share their insights with other groups. (interpersonal)

- Ask students to write a letter or a poem as if they were Saint Francis, responding to some current event in society or in school. (intrapersonal, linguistic)

- Studying various artistic representations of Saint Francis, ask students to explain the meaning of each one. (logical-mathematical, spatial, linguistic)

- Create gestures to accompany the "Prayer of Saint Francis;" learn the words to the prayer in the original Italian. (bodily-kinesthetic, linguistic)

RELIGION CLASS #7

Grade Level: Junior High
Topic: The Sacrament of the Anointing of the Sick
Objective: To sensitize students to the needs of the sick and the need for the Sacrament

Students will appreciate the special needs of sick people and the importance of the Sacrament of the Anointing of the Sick.

- Ask the students to recall and share a recent experience of sickness. (intrapersonal, interpersonal)

- Read a Gospel story about Jesus' care for the sick. (linguistic)

- Invite health care professional (nurse, doctor, pharmacist) to class to discuss the special circumstances surrounding illness. (interpersonal, logical-mathematical)

- Have students make cards or write letters to encourage the sick; visit a hospital or extended care facility to present them or sing a few inspirational songs. (spatial, bodily-kinesthetic, musical)

- Combine a science or health lesson with religion class on the theme of physical and spiritual health. (logical-mathematical)

RELIGION CLASS #8

Grade Level: High School
Topic: The Book of Revelation
Objective: To introduce students to apocalyptic literature

Students will understand the purpose of apocalyptic literature as a literature of resistance.

- Collect group ideas about the Book of Revelation, including what the students already know and questions they have. (linguistic)

- Have the class silently read a passage from Revelation (suggest Rev. 11:15-19) off an overhead transparency. (intrapersonal, linguistic)

- Demonstrate a dramatic reading of the passage for the class. (linguistic)

- Ask the students to draw or sketch a representation of the scene. (spatial)

- Play a triumphal piece of music, such as Aaron Copeland's *Fanfare for a Common Man,* while students are drawing. (musical)

- Invite students to "conduct" an imaginary orchestra as the music plays. (bodily-kinesthetic)

- Share student drawings with each other, and have them explain why they drew what they did. (interpersonal)

- Give the class other examples of literature of resistance; compare and contrast these with Revelation. (logical-mathematical)

- Compose journal entries about what it felt like to live during a time of religious persecution. (intrapersonal, linguistic)

RELIGION CLASS #9

Grade Level: High School
Topic: The humanity of Jesus
Objective: To demonstrate that Jesus was human and had feelings.

Students will understand and appreciate the humanity of Jesus by studying and reflecting on various images of Jesus in the New Testament.

- Ask students what makes human beings different from other animals. (logical-mathematical)

- Have the students read different Gospel accounts of Jesus' healing miracles in small groups. (linguistic, interpersonal)

- Ask students how they would feel if confronted with serious sickness, injury or death of a loved one. (intrapersonal)

- Read the Gospel account of the raising of Lazarus to the class. (linguistic)

- Discuss the funeral and burial practices of New Testament times. (linguistic, logical-mathematical, interpersonal)

- Watch the segment of the raising of Lazarus from the film "Jesus of Nazareth." (spatial)

- Play several liturgical hymns and analyze their lyrics and verses for evidence of Jesus' feelings. Some suggestions are *The Cry of the Poor, Mighty Lord,* and *The King of Love.* (musical)

- Summarize the various feelings of Jesus by use of facial gestures or charades. (bodily-kinesthetic)

RELIGION CLASS #10

Level: Adult
Topic: Introduction to Theology
Objective: To introduce participants to theological methodology

Participants will understand and appreciate various ways of learning about theology.

- Explain the etymology of the term "theology." (linguistic)

- Ask the class to think about their early childhood images of God; invite them to share that image with one other person. (intrapersonal, interpersonal)

- Read several classical examples from the saints or from theologians about their understanding of God, then ask the class to compare their experiences with the ones described in the readings. (linguistic, logical-mathematical)

- Visit several churches, or show photographs or slides of different churches, traditional and modern. Compare and contrast a Gothic cathedral to a modern, newly constructed church. What does the architecture say about who God is? (spatial)

- Analyze the various postures used at Mass: standing, sitting, kneeling, open arms (orans position), bowing, genuflecting, etc. What does each action suggest about God? (bodily-kinesthetic)

- Play and sing several liturgical hymns, again contrasting old and new. Compare the traditional *Praise to the Lord* with the more contemporary *Blessed Be the Lord*. What image of God is revealed in each song? (musical)

- Display various artistic representations of God from different historical periods. Have the class comment on the image of God each portrays. (spatial, logical-mathematical, interpersonal)

- Ask the participants to select their favorite church, liturgical hymn, painting, posture, and theological description of God. (intrapersonal)

RELIGION CLASS #11

Level: Adult
Topic: Community
Objective: To see the Church as community

Participants will understand and experience the Church as a community of faith.

- Sing the Quaker hymn, *Simple Gifts*, and dance in a circle in unison. (musical, bodily-kinesthetic)

- Have participants work on a word puzzle or jumble of religious vocabulary words alone, then invite them into groups. (linguistic, interpersonal)

- Read Acts 2: 42-47 and other Scriptures on the unity of the early Christian communities, then ask participants to reflect on their meaning. (linguistic, intrapersonal)

- Have participants work in pairs to build a house of cards. (spatial, interpersonal)

- Work together on a capital improvement project for a neighbor in need, such as painting, trimming hedges or raking leaves. (bodily-kinesthetic, interpersonal)

- Ask participants to consider the similarities between New Testament communities and today's churches. (logical-mathematical)

- Show a video or have a guest speaker on small Christian communities or the base communities of Latin America. (spatial, interpersonal)

- Plan a prayer service around the theme "The Body of Christ," using First Corinthians 12 as the focus. (interpersonal, linguistic, intrapersonal, musical)

RELIGION CLASS #12

Level: Married Couples
Topic: Love & fidelity
Objective: To nurture the relationships of married couples

Participants will reflect on their married life and strengthen their marriage relationship.

- Read the Gospel story of the wedding feast at Cana. (linguistic)

- Invite couples to share one story from their wedding. (interpersonal)

- Ask couples to create three story problems about married life based on their experience that would be helpful for engaged couples to consider. (logical-mathematical)

- Have couples draw a time-line, charting the history of their relationship, and graphing important events. (spatial)

- Ask individual spouses to write letters to each other around a theme of mutual agreement. (intrapersonal)

- Have each couple sing a song that was played at their wedding, was their favorite or was popular when they were married. (musical)

- Conclude with a square dance. (bodily-kinesthetic)

ENHANCEMENT STRATEGIES

One of the exciting ramifications about using multiple intelligence theory for one class is that teachers soon start adapting the theory to other classes and activities. The beauty of MI theory is that many of the skills, techniques and approaches used for one subject area are easily transferable to others. Thus, once students are comfortable with the theory and the seven ways of knowing, they come to expect a diversity of classroom activities and anticipate being challenged and engaged in similar ways in all subjects. Some useful MI strategies, applicable across the curriculum, are:

Linguistic

- brainstorming ideas, questions, and what students already know at the beginning of a new unit
- repeating a homework assignment in pairs to assure everyone understands what is expected
- quizzing each other on new vocabulary and spelling
- debates, trivia games and other content-based group activities
- summarizing a lesson with a single word or creating a mnemonic device

Musical

- use musical vocabulary to give directions; slow the tempo of the reading; get the group to work in harmony; no solo productions
- use music to create or enhance the desired atmosphere for a lesson
- stay current with music popular with the students and look for themes and issues that may be relevant to the curriculum
- encourage students to write their own songs or to write new lyrics for known songs based on classroom learning
- play, analyze and evaluate pre-recorded music about a subject area

Logical-Mathematical

- ask students to connect or relate new learning to previous learning
- have students invent word or story problems about new material
- have students do surveys and interviews outside of class related to classroom activities
- play questioning games such as "20 Questions"
- always ask "why?"

Spatial

- summarize new learning by making posters, collages, graphs, charts or other displays
- use computer graphics, drawing programs and *Hypercard* applications to encourage students to demonstrate their learning
- make a videotape of learning activities, a photograph display or a slide show
- use diagrams, charts and visual organizers to show the relationships between lessons
- use color as an organizer for categories

Bodily-Kinesthetic

- plan regular field trips that include hands-on activities
- use role play, simulation exercises and other content-based games
- use athletic activities and metaphors as teaching tools; for example, bowling pins for lists of ten and a baseball diamond for four items
- use and construct manipulatives appropriate to the lesson
- develop charade and pantomime activities to summarize a lesson

Interpersonal

- cooperative learning groups or cooperative pairs to work together on projects
- peer teaching activities where students teach each other a part of a lesson
- work together on projects outside of the classroom that benefit the school, parish or local community
- invite guest speakers, outside experts, or local leaders to visit a class when appropriate
- develop a pattern for small group discussions on topics and a way to report the results of such discussions to the whole class

Intrapersonal

- have students keep a reflective journal where they write regularly about what they are learning and its significance to them
- engage students in a goal-setting exercise at the beginning of each year, semester or class
- vary assessment techniques to include student portfolios and multimedia
- incorporate independent learning activities and self-designed study projects into the curriculum
- develop vehicles for students to engage in regular self-assessment

GETTING STARTED

Change often comes slowly in any organization, and the first step is typically the most difficult. More than anything else, fear is what drives the resistance to try something new. In an effort to address and anticipate some of those fears associated with all things new, the following ideas are offered to ease the transition to a multiple intelligences educational environment.

Teach the Theory Itself

A necessary first step to multiple intelligence teaching techniques is to teach the basics of the theory to students, staff and parents. Thomas Armstrong noted that one of the most useful characteristics of MI theory is that it can be explained to just about any student in a relatively short period of time. Following an age-appropriate grasp of the theory, students can then easily proceed to make use of MI vocabulary and images to describe, evaluate and reflect upon their learning.

It is important for parents to understand the background of the theory and to appreciate the diversity of pedagogy that MI thinking invites. If parents are accustomed to a traditional classroom setting where most teaching is teacher-directed and highly verbal, they may not at first understand the value of a different approach. Explaining the variety of intelligences, and the implications for classroom practice as well as helping parents reflect on their own learning styles, will assist in broadening popular opinion about what constitutes good teaching.

Prepare the Classroom

A classroom organized with individual student desks in neat, parallel rows all facing in the direction of the teacher is not conducive to MI teaching. Such a structure indicates by its very design that learning is an isolated, individual activity done alone, albeit alongside others who are working alone. It suggests that teaching is primarily a function of what the teacher says and does, and that nothing is more important than listening to the teacher lecture. In such an environment, any MI lesson will be out of place.

Some teachers have had success in implementing MI theory by designing MI centers in the classroom for each of the intelligences. Each center can be designed in such a way as to facilitate the particular intelligence in question and appropriate materials and supplies can be located there. Bruce Campbell suggests in his recent, *The Multiple Intelligences Handbook*, that each of the MI centers be given names. Naming the center for an individual provides a concrete experience of the value of that intelligence and gives the students a type of "mentor in absentia." Campbell further noted that the naming gives students a concrete role model for that intelligence. Thus, the musical center can be called the Beethoven Center. One teacher observed that students sometimes described a classmate who showed a particularly strong ability in one area by referring to the title of the center. For example, "she's a modern day Beethoven."

In this spirit, some possibilities for MI centers in religious education include:

Linguistic	Thomas Aquinas Center
Musical	Sr. Thea Bowman Center
Logical-Mathematical	Leonardo DaVinci Center
Spatial	Michelangelo Center
Bodily-Kinesthetic	St. Joseph Center
Interpersonal	Mother Teresa Center
intrapersonal	St. Teresa of Avila Center

Campbell reported that several teachers have experimented with other ways to name their MI centers, including naming them after teachers in the building, fictional characters and members in the local community. Thus, in a high school setting, the centers may look like this:

Linguistic	[Name of English Teacher] Center
Musical	[Name of Band Director] Center
Logical-Mathematical	[Name of Math Teacher] Center
Spatial	[Name of Art Teacher] Center
Bodily-Kinesthetic	[Name of Physical Education Teacher] Center
Interpersonal	[Name of Guidance Counselor] Center
Intrapersonal	[Name of School Chaplain] Center

The center names can be changed during the course of the year in response to events or to developments in the curriculum.

Gather Intelligence: Appropriate Materials and Resources

Having materials and resources appropriate to each intelligence is an important component of successful implementation of MI theory. Many of the materials mentioned here are readily obtainable in the typical school or home. Others will require purchase. While it is not necessary to assemble a treasure chest of resources before beginning, experienced teachers know well the importance of the availability of proper materials. Some useful materials for implementing MI teaching strategies for each intelligence are:

Linguistic
textbooks, including Bibles
magazines
encyclopedias
dictionaries, thesauruses
newspapers
paper and pencils
computer and printer
word processing software

Logical-Mathematical
manipulatives
attendance data
puzzles
games
measuring instruments
graphs

Bodily-Kinesthetic
religious items
costumes
sports equipment
art supplies
puppets

Intrapersonal
candle
kneeler (priedieux)
bean bags
head phones
prayer space or rug

Musical
portable stereo system
records
CDs
cassettes
portable keyboard
musical instruments
sheet music
song books

Spatial
art & craft supplies
religious art
videos
photographs, slides
maps
flash cards

Interpersonal
student mailboxes
tables
cooperative games & projects
face-to-face seating
lives of the saints books

CHAPTER IV
MULTIPLE INTELLIGENCE
THEORY AND THE MASS

THE MASS YESTERDAY AND TODAY

One of the often quoted lines of the Second Vatican Council concerns its observations about the place of the liturgy in the life of the Church. It reads, "still, the liturgy is the summit toward which the activity of the Church is directed; at the same time it is the fount from which all the Church's power flows." Taken from paragraph #10 of the Constitution on the Liturgy, *Sacrosanctum Concilium*, these words introduced a period of tremendous renewal in the Church. The Constitution on the Liturgy was the first of the documents promulgated by Vatican II, heeding its own advice that the celebration of the Eucharist is where the Church both begins and reaches its zenith. The eucharistic sacrifice, the Mass, is both the source and summit of ecclesial life.

For more than three decades now, Catholics around the world have embraced this exalted view of the place of eucharistic worship in their lives. Perhaps in no other area of ecclesial life has the Church witnessed the energy, excitement and renewal of spirit so profoundly as in the liturgical renaissance. While liturgical innovations continue to be criticized in some circles, there is general agreement that the liturgical renewal begun at Vatican II paved the way for a whole new understanding of Church. Admittedly, the transition period was difficult. Liturgical forms and structures have continued to evolve, to the delight of some and the consternation of others. In the end, Catholics care deeply about their eucharistic worship because it is the focal point and zenith of the Christian life.

Of the many changes in practice and in theology introduced by Vatican II, one simple observation stands out. Believers began to think of themselves as the Church, and the Church was understood to be holy. "We are the Church." Such was the cry of the people of God following the Council. Echoing another document of Vatican II, the Dogmatic Constitution on the Church, *Lumen Gentium*, the operative definition of the Church became "the people of God," or, as *Lumen Gentium* declares, "the holy people of God (paragraph #12)." The Church was holy. The people of God are the Church. The people of God are holy. While this may seem like a facile theological reconstruction of very complicated ideas, its simplicity is jarring. The people of God are a holy people.

This fundamental insight of ecclesial self-identity was to have a profound impact on worship. Before Vatican II, it can safely be stated that people came to Mass and the sacraments to taste holiness and experience the infusion of the divine into their otherwise secular lives. The believing community typically judged itself sinful, unworthy, profane. The necessity for worship, sacraments and grace was very much nurtured by that sinful self-perception. God was in large part absent from daily life, but Mass and the sacraments made God present. One came to Mass to acquire what could not be found elsewhere in life: God.

By calling attention to the holiness of the Church and, therefore, to the holiness of the people, Vatican II shifted a focus of liturgical prayer. The Mass remained the way of following the Lord's command—of making Christ present. The Church persisted in its conviction of the real and abiding presence of Christ in the Eucharist. But the celebration of the Mass and the structure of worship, became more people-oriented. It became more of an activity of the community and less of an individual's exercise for God. While remaining a powerful expression of God's goodness and presence, the Mass became a celebration of the community. Since the community was holy and since it was the Church, it followed that its corporate prayer would itself be sanctifying.

Another way of looking at this development is to consider the vertical and horizontal dimensions. Prior to Vatican II, liturgical prayer was a predominantly vertical experience. Worship was prayer directed to God, from earth to heaven. The Mass itself was very much a function of the priest who, on behalf of the people, directed this vertical prayer to God.

While there is no denying that all prayer assumes some form of vertical direction, the renewed liturgy brings to life a myriad of horizontal structures that call attention to the holiness of God's people and to God's presence not only in heaven, but also in the faithful. Dialogical prayers; the responses, both spoken and sung; the offering of gifts; the exchange of peace; and the various ministries—all of these indicate and in fact celebrate the abiding presence of God in the lives of the people. One does not watch or attend Mass anymore. The *congregation* no longer *hears* Mass. The Church celebrates the Eucharist. The community gathers to celebrate the wonders God has done. By reflecting on their life together, through hearing God's word and by struggling to connect the two, people of faith struggle to discern and interpret the ongoing revelation of God in their lives. Thus, there is an active horizontal dimension that animates the eucharistic assembly.

God is no longer thought absent or distant, but very much present in the lives of the people. Liturgical prayer is not a question of God's presence to the people. Rather, it is the people's attentiveness to God that is in question and needs to be challenged. The liturgy directs and assists the people of God to name and lift up the constant and unwavering relationship that God has with the Church. Here lies the beauty of the Mass. Such communal worship is the source and summit of the Christian life. It calls the people of God to be fully who they are: holy. It challenges the Church to remember its origin: God. It points the Church to its final destiny: God. Through the celebration of the Eucharist, the people of God come to experience and manifest their beginning as well as their end.

Understood as a community action, the Mass is a celebration of who the Church is, where it came from, and where it is going. It represents and embodies the essential characteristics of what it means to be the people of God. It should come as no surprise that such a gathering and celebration would speak to every dimension of the human being and engage the giftedness of the community on a variety of levels.

The wisdom of Catholic tradition is abundantly evident in the structure of the Mass. Why? Because as it is now structured, the Mass is a veritable festival of the human spirit, calling forth the rich blessings that the people of God have graciously received. If Gardner is correct in his assessment that all people have at least seven intelligences, then there is no environment more conducive to engaging these intelligences than the Mass. The Mass, quite simply, has them all. While even the seasoned religion teacher may have to struggle at first to implement MI theory in the classroom, the Mass calls forth all of the intelligences and unifies MI theory in a highly experiential way.

This is not to suggest a competition between liturgical practice and pedagogical theory, nor is it a matter of the priority of one over the other. The Mass, in various forms, has been a part of Catholic practice for centuries. MI theory is a little more than a decade old. But what is clearly seen here is a strong resonance between a contemporary theory of human intelligence and a biblically-based, time-honored communal prayer form. Liturgists and theologians need not be concerned that more is being read into the structure of the Mass than is really there, for the Mass, as the current official texts prescribe it, contains clear directives that engage the seven intelligences. MI advocates and educators should not be concerned that someone is simply "baptizing" a sound theory and giving it religious significance. On the contrary, the long-standing power of the Mass in Catholic history, its pride of place in the tradition, its being the source and summit of the Church's life, all lend credence to its structure and its engagement of a multiplicity of human gifts. In short, the Mass is history's longest running example of the effectiveness of MI theory in action. Of course, this is somewhat anachronistic. The early Church, and the majority of Catholics in history knew nothing of MI theory. Perhaps the recent advent of MI theory is a step in explaining why countless generations of believers have found the Mass integral to their faith.

Think for a moment of the various activities that accompany the ordinary Sunday Mass. Song is a must. People are invited to sing in unison, listen prayerfully to reflective pieces or respond to an antiphonal arrangement. The faithful stand, sit, kneel, bow, genuflect and bless themselves. At different times during the liturgy there is dialogue with the celebrant. At other times there is a respectful, reverential silence. There is a corporate movement toward the altar for communion, a shared greeting at the sign of peace, and more often than not a ritualized leave-taking of each other at the church doors. There are appropriate costumes for those involved in the drama, and color is a major part of the ambience. Most importantly, there is an order and logic to the celebration on which believers come to depend. For the most part, Catholics know what to expect when they go to Mass. It is precisely in that comfort zone, in that familiarity with the liturgical rites, that the Mass displays its most awesome power.

Children's liturgies are another good example of how the Mass engages many dimensions of the human spirit. It has become commonplace for children to dramatize a certain reading from the Scriptures, learn or create gestures to a song or the Lord's Prayer and sing their hearts out in lively, invigorating melodies. Experiencing the spiritual power of such liturgies, many have grown attached to the beauty and simplicity of child-like faith.

Whether it is exclusively with children or the broader Sunday assembly, the Mass appeals to and utilizes a wide variety of human gifts. In fact, looking at each of the parts of the Mass, we can see each intelligence engaged in a general way simply by celebrating the Eucharist as it is prescribed in the *Roman Missal*.

CELEBRATING THE MASS

The Introductory Rites

The overriding purpose of the Introductory Rites is to unify all those present into a community. While the people may come as individuals or as individual units, the prayer of the Mass is a corporate, communal prayer. The people of God is one people, united in one voice, to praise the one God. What a perfect way to unite the community—by giving them one voice in song and in response. When the faithful join in song and in response to dialogical greetings and prayers, their unity is palpable.

Musical intelligence is highly utilized throughout the Mass, beginning with the opening hymn or gathering song. This is really not the beginning of the community's prayer, however. The act of coming into a space, getting settled and situated and becoming comfortable is a necessary part of properly joining in the prayer. Why is it that certain families and individual's tend to occupy the same seat or bench on Sundays? Why do classes sit together at school liturgies and always in the same place? Why is it that some find it difficult to focus if, because of circumstances beyond their control, they must sit on the opposite side of the aisle from their usual seat, thereby getting a new angle or view? All of these answers involve spatial intelligence and the ability to find one's place in the physical environment. Spatial intelligence also comes into play before the liturgy begins in the preparation of the worship space. The arrangement of furniture and flowers, banners and colors, all suggest the importance of making the space conducive for the action that will follow. Even the design and architectural structure of the church conveys a certain theological perspective about who God is and God's relationship to the people.

Churches that have greeters and ushers attend to interpersonal needs as the faithful are welcomed upon arrival and made to feel at home. In many places, it is customary, once the faithful are spatially oriented and settled in their seats, to offer a short, private, quiet prayer to God. This experience is highly intrapersonal and has the effect of centering one's self on God and the worship that follows. More traditional believers would not have progressed this far without having had already blessed themselves with holy water. A genuflection might have preceded the taking of one's seat. These activities address the  bodily-kinesthetic intelligence, as does kneeling. Mass has yet to begin and already the worship experience is engaging the faithful on a variety of levels.

The dialogue, prayers, biblical greeting, penitential rite and responses that make up the Introductory Rites also help to prepare the assembly to be attentive to God's word and to celebrate the Eucharist. The fact that they are called Introductory Rites suggests that this is an experience that points to another activity, and not an end in itself. For this reason, the Introductory Rites are brief. However, they follow a certain pattern and logically serve an important purpose. They mark the beginning of the assembly's prayer and orient the faithful to God's word and the Lord's table.

Liturgy of the Word

The readings from the Scriptures predominantly make use of linguistic intelligence. Whether listening attentively or following along from a printed text, the faithful turn their attention to words, in spoken and written form, as a meditation on the presence of God.

The Liturgy of the Word also includes the responsorial psalm and gospel acclamation, both of which are best expressed in song. Musical intelligence is important here, but the structure of the responsorial psalm and gospel acclamation also involve the faithful in dialogical responses, where a song leader, cantor or choir sing, and the assembly responds. This communication, albeit musical, is also interpersonal. The assembly's posture should not go unnoticed here either, as the sitting receptivity of the first and second readings is transformed into attentive standing and gospel respect. The bodily-kinesthetic dimension to various postures is a powerful expression of and support for the action of the liturgy. The threefold blessing with the cross during the dialogue which greets the gospel reading is another bodily-kinesthetic support for what the liturgy is trying to accomplish.

The purpose of the homily is to explain the readings and to apply their message to the lives of the assembly. Good homilies are inspired by, related to and logically connected to the readings. Thus, listening to a good homily is going to put the assembly into a dialogue with the readings. In this sense, the homily is much more than a linguistic expression of the preacher. It is a logical, interpersonal communication between the assembly and God's word. Linguistic, logical, and interpersonal intelligence are required. Many presiders conclude the homily with a short period of silence to allow for reflection and consideration of what was said. Such a silence calls forth an intrapersonal movement through which believers may do some heartfelt introspection.

The profession of faith is a highly verbal, linguistic affirmation of faith on the part of the assembly. Recitation of any creed from memory requires a certain degree of linguistic skill. Both the Apostles' Creed and the Nicene Creed follow a type of chronological order in recalling the great events in salvation history. The recognition of the order and the proper sequencing of the creedal events necessitate a logical, mathematical reasoning.

The petitions, or Prayers of the Faithful, represent spoken prayers for the needs of the faithful and for all. Several intelligences are expressed here. The structure of each prayer calls for a response from the assembly, thus creating an interpersonal environment. The nature of the prayers for others and those beyond the immediate community call for a global awareness that is the epitome of interpersonal intelligence. Prayers for one's own community or for local needs require a healthy self-awareness of anxieties or shortcomings that is properly described as intrapersonal intelligence. Often commu-nities allow a period or prayer of silence for individual's to express the "needs of their hearts," thus calling upon intrapersonal intelligence again. Others invite individual members of the faithful to give voice to their own intentions. In any event, the petitions clearly go beyond the simple linguistic articulation of needs. The very nature of this ritual prayer is alternately interpersonal and intrapersonal.

Liturgy of the Eucharist

The Eucharistic Prayer, the great prayer of thanksgiving, is the focal point of the celebration. The prayer begins with the Preface, introduced by a dialogue between presider and assembly that is highly interpersonal. The preface itself invites a response, the *Sanctus*, typically sung and calling forth musical intelligence.

While the bulk of the prayer from the *Sanctus* forward is often a spoken prayer of the presider and highly linguistic, the nature of the ritual and the built-in acclamations offer a considerable degree of engagement of the other intelligences. For example, all of the Eucharistic Prayers contain references to the life and ministry of Jesus, recalling especially his meal behaviors the night before he died. Specifically, the prayers recount his sharing bread and wine with his followers and his commanding them to do the same in his memory. For most Christians, these words are familiar and are easily associated with mental images and pictures. The telling and retelling of the story, therefore, involves spatial intelligence in that engaged listeners often supply a mental picture of the event.

The structure of the ritual, its reliance on the repetition of certain forms, and the recalling of the central events of the faith over and over again give the liturgy a stability and a security that is often elusive in life. This is not to say that the liturgy is never novel or challenging; it is simply to suggest that the familiarity of liturgical prayer forms creates a comfort zone for the assembly because they come to rely on and to expect certain words, actions, responses and songs. This personal history of expectation that each one brings to the assembly is based on a logical-mathematical intelligence.

Posture is also an issue during the Eucharistic Prayer. This bodily-kinesthetic dimension to prayer provides a significant support for the assembly in its effort to focus on God. Whether kneeling or standing, the assembly is focused totally and completely on the act of thanksgiving. Visually, the assembly looks to the altar, to the outstretched arms of the presider, to the elements on the table. Musically, the praises of God are proclaimed. Incense maybe used to create special aromas that draw attention to the fact that this is a sacred space and a sacred time. The people of God sit, stand, kneel, bow, respond and sing, and thereby engage many dimensions of the human spirit.

The eucharistic acclamations provide a way for the assembly to respond to the outpouring of God's grace and to affirm their faith. Usually sung, these short responses invite a musical, interpersonal dialogue that brings life and festivity to the prayer. In children's liturgies, the Eucharistic Prayers contain a variety of such responses and are, in fact, structured around the acclamations of the assembly. Such frequent use of sung responses makes the prayer less verbal and abstract, and more amenable to children. All of the eucharistic acclamations—the *Sanctus*, Memorial Acclamation, Great Amen, and the children's acclamations—call forth a variety of intelligences. Musical, interpersonal, linguistic and logical intelligence are necessary at different times and in varying ways.

The Communion Rite is the climax of the liturgy and reaches full expression when the assembly eats and drinks the body and blood of the Lord. The beauty of the entire liturgy and especially of the Communion Rite is evident as the ritual calls forth the total attention and dedication of the assembly. The Communion Rite begins with the Lord's Prayer, done in unison following Jesus' command. Whether recited or sung, the prayer recalls Jesus' own approach to prayer and to God and proclaims a theology and a cosmology for the Christian life. Many assemblies introduce a bodily-kinesthetic experience to this normally linguistic or musical expression by inviting the assembly to join hands or by teaching the assembly prayerful gestures to accompany the prayer.

The Rite of Peace is at once interpersonal and bodily-kinesthetic, typically taking the form of an offer of a handshake accompanied by a verbal greeting of peace. It is preceded by a dialogical greeting with the presider that reminds the assembly that the peace it shares has its origins in God.

The Lamb of God and the Fraction Rite are intended to be highly symbolic actions that visually give shape to the community's prayer. The breaking of the bread and pouring of the wine are the primary eucharistic symbols. The rubrics encourage the use of one large piece of bread and one large cup or other vessel to hold wine for the entire assembly. Thus, it is important that this action is clearly seen and not somehow lost or hidden on the altar. The broken bread and poured wine are symbols of Christ and what Christ offered for God's people. The dialogical responses of the Lamb of God and the invitation to communion provide an interpersonal context as the distribution of communion begins.

There is an important spatial and bodily-kinesthetic dynamic to the entire communion experience. The assembly approaches the altar, assumes a reverent posture to eat and drink and returns to its original position. Interpersonal dialogue with the communion minister is an anticipated part of this ritual. Song usually accompanies this procession. Many communicants return to their places to offer a silent prayer of thanksgiving. Nearly every intelligence is engaged in the communion rite as the ritual itself reaches out to every aspect of the human person. The total person is engaged and graced, and properly so, for this is the source and summit of the Christian life. The dignity and wisdom of eucharistic prayer has never before been realized in such terms or through such a lens, but it is true nonetheless. The culmination of Mass in the Communion Rite, with the people of God partaking of the Lord's body and blood, is truly a celebration of the multiple intelligences. Engaged throughout the entire liturgy, the multiple human intelligences reach their zenith in the Communion Rite.

The entire Mass, while rooted in the long standing tradition of the church, is a showcase for the multiple human intelligences. Is it any wonder that, when properly planned and celebrated, the Mass can be a moving experience for people of faith? Given Gardner's theory, it is easy to understand why: the Mass engages and celebrates every aspect of human giftedness.

BIBLIOGRAPHY

Armstrong, Thomas. *Multiple Intelligences in the Classroom*. Alexandria, VA: ASCD, 1994.

Armstrong, Thomas. *Seven Kinds of Smart*. New York: Plume/Penguin, 1993.

Bodo, Murray. *Song of the Sparrow*. Cincinnati: St. Anthony Messenger, 1976.

Bruetsch, Anne. *Multiple Intelligences Lesson Plan Book*. Tucson, AZ: Zephyr Press, 1995.

Butler, Alban. *Lives of the Saints*. San Francisco: Harper & Row, 1985.

Campbell, Bruce. *The Multiple Intelligences Handbook*. Stanwood, WA: Campbell & Assoc., 1994.

Catholic Church, *Roman Missal*. Collegeville, MN: The Liturgical Press, 1985.

Copland, Aaron. *Fanfare for a Common Man* in *The Copland Collection: Copland Conducts Copland*. Sony Corporation: DIDC 070791, SM3K 36550, disc #1, track #4.

Flannery, Austin, O.P. (Ed.). *Vatican Council II: The Conciliar and Post Conciliar Documents*. Northport, NY: Costello Publishing Co., 1987.

Gardner, Howard. *Frames of Mind*. New York: Basic Books, 1985.

Lazear, David. *Seven Pathways of Learning: Teaching Students and Parents About Multiple Intelligences*. Tucson, AZ: Zephyr Press, 1994.

Lazear, David. *Seven Ways of Knowing: Teaching for Multiple Intelligences*. Pallatine, IL: Skylight Publishing, 1991.

Lazear, David. *Seven Ways of Teaching: The Artistry of Teaching with Multiple Intelligences*. Pallatine, IL: Skylight Publishing, 1991.

Lazear, David. *Teaching for Multiple Intelligences*. Bloomington, IN: Phi Delta Kappa Educational Foundation, 1992.

New American Bible. New York: Catholic Book Publishing Company, 1970.